BOWLING

BOWLING SCORE RECORD

Name	1	2	3	4	5	6	7	8	9	10	Total
1											
2											
3											
4											
5											
6											
7											
8											
9											
10											
11											
12											
13											
14											
15											
16											

Date :	Lanes :

Bowling Score Sheet

Name	1	2	3	4	5	6	7	8	9	10	Total
1											
2											
3											
4											
5											
6											
7											
8											
9											
10											
11											
12											
13											
14											
15											
16											

Date :	Lanes :

Bowling Score Sheet

Name	1	2	3	4	5	6	7	8	9	10	Total
1											
2											
3											
4											
5											
6											
7											
8											
9											
10											
11											
12											
13											
14											
15											
16											

Date :	Lanes :

Bowling Score Sheet

Name	1	2	3	4	5	6	7	8	9	10	Total
1											
2											
3											
4											
5											
6											
7											
8											
9											
10											
11											
12											
13											
14											
15											
16											

Date :	Lanes :

Bowling Score Sheet

Name	1	2	3	4	5	6	7	8	9	10	Total
1											
2											
3											
4											
5											
6											
7											
8											
9											
10											
11											
12											
13											
14											
15											
16											

Date :	Lanes :

Bowling Score Sheet

Name	1	2	3	4	5	6	7	8	9	10	Total
1											
2											
3											
4											
5											
6											
7											
8											
9											
10											
11											
12											
13											
14											
15											
16											

Date :	Lanes :

Bowling Score Sheet

Name	1	2	3	4	5	6	7	8	9	10	Total
1											
2											
3											
4											
5											
6											
7											
8											
9											
10											
11											
12											
13											
14											
15											
16											

Date :	Lanes :

Bowling Score Sheet

Name	1	2	3	4	5	6	7	8	9	10	Total
1											
2											
3											
4											
5											
6											
7											
8											
9											
10											
11											
12											
13											
14											
15											
16											

Date :	Lanes :

Bowling Score Sheet

Name	1	2	3	4	5	6	7	8	9	10	Total
1											
2											
3											
4											
5											
6											
7											
8											
9											
10											
11											
12											
13											
14											
15											
16											

Date :	Lanes :

Bowling Score Sheet

Name	1	2	3	4	5	6	7	8	9	10	Total
1											
2											
3											
4											
5											
6											
7											
8											
9											
10											
11											
12											
13											
14											
15											
16											

Date :	Lanes :

Bowling Score Sheet

Name	1	2	3	4	5	6	7	8	9	10	Total
1											
2											
3											
4											
5											
6											
7											
8											
9											
10											
11											
12											
13											
14											
15											
16											

Date :	Lanes :

Bowling Score Sheet

Name	1	2	3	4	5	6	7	8	9	10	Total
1											
2											
3											
4											
5											
6											
7											
8											
9											
10											
11											
12											
13											
14											
15											
16											

Date :	Lanes :

Bowling Score Sheet

Name	1	2	3	4	5	6	7	8	9	10	Total
1											
2											
3											
4											
5											
6											
7											
8											
9											
10											
11											
12											
13											
14											
15											
16											

Date :	Lanes :

Bowling Score Sheet

Name	1	2	3	4	5	6	7	8	9	10	Total
1											
2											
3											
4											
5											
6											
7											
8											
9											
10											
11											
12											
13											
14											
15											
16											

Date :	Lanes :

Bowling Score Sheet

Name	1	2	3	4	5	6	7	8	9	10	Total
1											
2											
3											
4											
5											
6											
7											
8											
9											
10											
11											
12											
13											
14											
15											
16											

Date :	Lanes :

Bowling Score Sheet

Name	1	2	3	4	5	6	7	8	9	10	Total
1											
2											
3											
4											
5											
6											
7											
8											
9											
10											
11											
12											
13											
14											
15											
16											

Date :	Lanes :

Bowling Score Sheet

Name	1	2	3	4	5	6	7	8	9	10	Total
1											
2											
3											
4											
5											
6											
7											
8											
9											
10											
11											
12											
13											
14											
15											
16											

Date :	Lanes :

Bowling Score Sheet

Name	1	2	3	4	5	6	7	8	9	10	Total
1											
2											
3											
4											
5											
6											
7											
8											
9											
10											
11											
12											
13											
14											
15											
16											

Date :	Lanes :

Bowling Score Sheet

Name	1	2	3	4	5	6	7	8	9	10	Total
1											
2											
3											
4											
5											
6											
7											
8											
9											
10											
11											
12											
13											
14											
15											
16											

Date :	Lanes :

Bowling Score Sheet

Name	1	2	3	4	5	6	7	8	9	10	Total
1											
2											
3											
4											
5											
6											
7											
8											
9											
10											
11											
12											
13											
14											
15											
16											

Date :	Lanes :

Bowling Score Sheet

Name	1	2	3	4	5	6	7	8	9	10	Total
1											
2											
3											
4											
5											
6											
7											
8											
9											
10											
11											
12											
13											
14											
15											
16											

Date :	Lanes :

Bowling Score Sheet

Name	1	2	3	4	5	6	7	8	9	10	Total
1											
2											
3											
4											
5											
6											
7											
8											
9											
10											
11											
12											
13											
14											
15											
16											

Date :	Lanes :

Bowling Score Sheet

Name	1	2	3	4	5	6	7	8	9	10	Total
1											
2											
3											
4											
5											
6											
7											
8											
9											
10											
11											
12											
13											
14											
15											
16											

Date :	Lanes :

Bowling Score Sheet

Name	1	2	3	4	5	6	7	8	9	10	Total
1											
2											
3											
4											
5											
6											
7											
8											
9											
10											
11											
12											
13											
14											
15											
16											

Date :	Lanes :

Bowling Score Sheet

Name	1	2	3	4	5	6	7	8	9	10	Total
1											
2											
3											
4											
5											
6											
7											
8											
9											
10											
11											
12											
13											
14											
15											
16											

Date :	Lanes :

Bowling Score Sheet

Name	1	2	3	4	5	6	7	8	9	10	Total
1											
2											
3											
4											
5											
6											
7											
8											
9											
10											
11											
12											
13											
14											
15											
16											

Date :	Lanes :

Bowling Score Sheet

Name	1	2	3	4	5	6	7	8	9	10	Total
1											
2											
3											
4											
5											
6											
7											
8											
9											
10											
11											
12											
13											
14											
15											
16											

Date :	Lanes :

Bowling Score Sheet

Name	1	2	3	4	5	6	7	8	9	10	Total
1											
2											
3											
4											
5											
6											
7											
8											
9											
10											
11											
12											
13											
14											
15											
16											

Date :	Lanes :

Bowling Score Sheet

Name	1	2	3	4	5	6	7	8	9	10	Total
1											
2											
3											
4											
5											
6											
7											
8											
9											
10											
11											
12											
13											
14											
15											
16											

Date :	Lanes :

Bowling Score Sheet

Name	1	2	3	4	5	6	7	8	9	10	Total
1											
2											
3											
4											
5											
6											
7											
8											
9											
10											
11											
12											
13											
14											
15											
16											

Date :	Lanes :

Bowling Score Sheet

Name	1	2	3	4	5	6	7	8	9	10	Total
1											
2											
3											
4											
5											
6											
7											
8											
9											
10											
11											
12											
13											
14											
15											
16											

Date :	Lanes :

Bowling Score Sheet

Name	1	2	3	4	5	6	7	8	9	10	Total
1											
2											
3											
4											
5											
6											
7											
8											
9											
10											
11											
12											
13											
14											
15											
16											

Date :	Lanes :

Bowling Score Sheet

Name	1	2	3	4	5	6	7	8	9	10	Total
1											
2											
3											
4											
5											
6											
7											
8											
9											
10											
11											
12											
13											
14											
15											
16											

Date :	Lanes :

Bowling Score Sheet

Name	1	2	3	4	5	6	7	8	9	10	Total
1											
2											
3											
4											
5											
6											
7											
8											
9											
10											
11											
12											
13											
14											
15											
16											

Date :	Lanes :

Bowling Score Sheet

Name	1	2	3	4	5	6	7	8	9	10	Total
1											
2											
3											
4											
5											
6											
7											
8											
9											
10											
11											
12											
13											
14											
15											
16											

Date :	Lanes :

Bowling Score Sheet

Name	1	2	3	4	5	6	7	8	9	10	Total
1											
2											
3											
4											
5											
6											
7											
8											
9											
10											
11											
12											
13											
14											
15											
16											

Date :	Lanes :

Bowling Score Sheet

Name	1	2	3	4	5	6	7	8	9	10	Total
1											
2											
3											
4											
5											
6											
7											
8											
9											
10											
11											
12											
13											
14											
15											
16											

Date :	Lanes :

Bowling Score Sheet

Name	1	2	3	4	5	6	7	8	9	10	Total
1											
2											
3											
4											
5											
6											
7											
8											
9											
10											
11											
12											
13											
14											
15											
16											

Date :	Lanes :

Bowling Score Sheet

Name	1	2	3	4	5	6	7	8	9	10	Total
1											
2											
3											
4											
5											
6											
7											
8											
9											
10											
11											
12											
13											
14											
15											
16											

Date :	**Lanes :**

Bowling Score Sheet

Name	1	2	3	4	5	6	7	8	9	10	Total
1											
2											
3											
4											
5											
6											
7											
8											
9											
10											
11											
12											
13											
14											
15											
16											

Date :	Lanes :

Bowling Score Sheet

Name	1	2	3	4	5	6	7	8	9	10	Total
1											
2											
3											
4											
5											
6											
7											
8											
9											
10											
11											
12											
13											
14											
15											
16											

Date :	Lanes :

Bowling Score Sheet

Name	1	2	3	4	5	6	7	8	9	10	Total
1											
2											
3											
4											
5											
6											
7											
8											
9											
10											
11											
12											
13											
14											
15											
16											

Date :	Lanes :

Bowling Score Sheet

Name	1	2	3	4	5	6	7	8	9	10	Total
1											
2											
3											
4											
5											
6											
7											
8											
9											
10											
11											
12											
13											
14											
15											
16											

Date :	Lanes :

Bowling Score Sheet

Name	1	2	3	4	5	6	7	8	9	10	Total
1											
2											
3											
4											
5											
6											
7											
8											
9											
10											
11											
12											
13											
14											
15											
16											

Date :	Lanes :

Bowling Score Sheet

Name	1	2	3	4	5	6	7	8	9	10	Total
1											
2											
3											
4											
5											
6											
7											
8											
9											
10											
11											
12											
13											
14											
15											
16											

Date :	Lanes :

Bowling Score Sheet

Name	1	2	3	4	5	6	7	8	9	10	Total
1											
2											
3											
4											
5											
6											
7											
8											
9											
10											
11											
12											
13											
14											
15											
16											

Date :	Lanes :

Bowling Score Sheet

Name	1	2	3	4	5	6	7	8	9	10	Total
1											
2											
3											
4											
5											
6											
7											
8											
9											
10											
11											
12											
13											
14											
15											
16											

Date :	Lanes :

Bowling Score Sheet

Name	1	2	3	4	5	6	7	8	9	10	Total
1											
2											
3											
4											
5											
6											
7											
8											
9											
10											
11											
12											
13											
14											
15											
16											

Date :	Lanes :

Bowling Score Sheet

Name	1	2	3	4	5	6	7	8	9	10	Total
1											
2											
3											
4											
5											
6											
7											
8											
9											
10											
11											
12											
13											
14											
15											
16											

Date :	Lanes :

Bowling Score Sheet

Name	1	2	3	4	5	6	7	8	9	10	Total
1											
2											
3											
4											
5											
6											
7											
8											
9											
10											
11											
12											
13											
14											
15											
16											

Date :	Lanes :

Bowling Score Sheet

Name	1	2	3	4	5	6	7	8	9	10	Total
1											
2											
3											
4											
5											
6											
7											
8											
9											
10											
11											
12											
13											
14											
15											
16											

Date :	Lanes :

Bowling Score Sheet

Name	1	2	3	4	5	6	7	8	9	10	Total
1											
2											
3											
4											
5											
6											
7											
8											
9											
10											
11											
12											
13											
14											
15											
16											

Date :	Lanes :

Bowling Score Sheet

Name	1	2	3	4	5	6	7	8	9	10	Total
1											
2											
3											
4											
5											
6											
7											
8											
9											
10											
11											
12											
13											
14											
15											
16											

Date :	Lanes :

Bowling Score Sheet

Name	1	2	3	4	5	6	7	8	9	10	Total
1											
2											
3											
4											
5											
6											
7											
8											
9											
10											
11											
12											
13											
14											
15											
16											

Date :	**Lanes :**

Bowling Score Sheet

Name	1	2	3	4	5	6	7	8	9	10	Total
1											
2											
3											
4											
5											
6											
7											
8											
9											
10											
11											
12											
13											
14											
15											
16											

Date :	Lanes :

Bowling Score Sheet

Name	1	2	3	4	5	6	7	8	9	10	Total
1											
2											
3											
4											
5											
6											
7											
8											
9											
10											
11											
12											
13											
14											
15											
16											

Date :	Lanes :

Bowling Score Sheet

Name	1	2	3	4	5	6	7	8	9	10	Total
1											
2											
3											
4											
5											
6											
7											
8											
9											
10											
11											
12											
13											
14											
15											
16											

Date :	Lanes :

Bowling Score Sheet

Name	1	2	3	4	5	6	7	8	9	10	Total
1											
2											
3											
4											
5											
6											
7											
8											
9											
10											
11											
12											
13											
14											
15											
16											

Date :	Lanes :

Bowling Score Sheet

Name	1	2	3	4	5	6	7	8	9	10	Total
1											
2											
3											
4											
5											
6											
7											
8											
9											
10											
11											
12											
13											
14											
15											
16											

Date :	Lanes :

Bowling Score Sheet

Name	1	2	3	4	5	6	7	8	9	10	Total
1											
2											
3											
4											
5											
6											
7											
8											
9											
10											
11											
12											
13											
14											
15											
16											

Date :	Lanes :

Bowling Score Sheet

Name	1	2	3	4	5	6	7	8	9	10	Total
1											
2											
3											
4											
5											
6											
7											
8											
9											
10											
11											
12											
13											
14											
15											
16											

Date :	Lanes :

Bowling Score Sheet

Name	1	2	3	4	5	6	7	8	9	10	Total
1											
2											
3											
4											
5											
6											
7											
8											
9											
10											
11											
12											
13											
14											
15											
16											

Date :	Lanes :

Bowling Score Sheet

Name	1	2	3	4	5	6	7	8	9	10	Total
1											
2											
3											
4											
5											
6											
7											
8											
9											
10											
11											
12											
13											
14											
15											
16											

Date :	Lanes :

Bowling Score Sheet

Name	1	2	3	4	5	6	7	8	9	10	Total
1											
2											
3											
4											
5											
6											
7											
8											
9											
10											
11											
12											
13											
14											
15											
16											

Date :	Lanes :

Bowling Score Sheet

Name	1	2	3	4	5	6	7	8	9	10	Total
1											
2											
3											
4											
5											
6											
7											
8											
9											
10											
11											
12											
13											
14											
15											
16											

Date :	Lanes :

Bowling Score Sheet

Name	1	2	3	4	5	6	7	8	9	10	Total
1											
2											
3											
4											
5											
6											
7											
8											
9											
10											
11											
12											
13											
14											
15											
16											

Date :	Lanes :

Bowling Score Sheet

Name	1	2	3	4	5	6	7	8	9	10	Total
1											
2											
3											
4											
5											
6											
7											
8											
9											
10											
11											
12											
13											
14											
15											
16											

Date :	Lanes :

Bowling Score Sheet

Name	1	2	3	4	5	6	7	8	9	10	Total
1											
2											
3											
4											
5											
6											
7											
8											
9											
10											
11											
12											
13											
14											
15											
16											

Date :	Lanes :

Bowling Score Sheet

Name	1	2	3	4	5	6	7	8	9	10	Total
1											
2											
3											
4											
5											
6											
7											
8											
9											
10											
11											
12											
13											
14											
15											
16											

Date :	Lanes :

Bowling Score Sheet

Name	1	2	3	4	5	6	7	8	9	10	Total
1											
2											
3											
4											
5											
6											
7											
8											
9											
10											
11											
12											
13											
14											
15											
16											

Date :	Lanes :

Bowling Score Sheet

Name	1	2	3	4	5	6	7	8	9	10	Total
1											
2											
3											
4											
5											
6											
7											
8											
9											
10											
11											
12											
13											
14											
15											
16											

Date :	Lanes :

Bowling Score Sheet

Name	1	2	3	4	5	6	7	8	9	10	Total
1											
2											
3											
4											
5											
6											
7											
8											
9											
10											
11											
12											
13											
14											
15											
16											

Date :	Lanes :

Bowling Score Sheet

Name	1	2	3	4	5	6	7	8	9	10	Total
1											
2											
3											
4											
5											
6											
7											
8											
9											
10											
11											
12											
13											
14											
15											
16											

Date :	Lanes :

Bowling Score Sheet

Name	1	2	3	4	5	6	7	8	9	10	Total
1											
2											
3											
4											
5											
6											
7											
8											
9											
10											
11											
12											
13											
14											
15											
16											

Date :	Lanes :

Bowling Score Sheet

Name	1	2	3	4	5	6	7	8	9	10	Total
1											
2											
3											
4											
5											
6											
7											
8											
9											
10											
11											
12											
13											
14											
15											
16											

Date :	Lanes :

Bowling Score Sheet

Name	1	2	3	4	5	6	7	8	9	10	Total
1											
2											
3											
4											
5											
6											
7											
8											
9											
10											
11											
12											
13											
14											
15											
16											

Date :	Lanes :

Bowling Score Sheet

Name	1	2	3	4	5	6	7	8	9	10	Total
1											
2											
3											
4											
5											
6											
7											
8											
9											
10											
11											
12											
13											
14											
15											
16											

Date :	Lanes :

Bowling Score Sheet

Name	1	2	3	4	5	6	7	8	9	10	Total
1											
2											
3											
4											
5											
6											
7											
8											
9											
10											
11											
12											
13											
14											
15											
16											

Date :	Lanes :

Bowling Score Sheet

Name	1	2	3	4	5	6	7	8	9	10	Total
1											
2											
3											
4											
5											
6											
7											
8											
9											
10											
11											
12											
13											
14											
15											
16											

Date :	Lanes :

Bowling Score Sheet

Name	1	2	3	4	5	6	7	8	9	10	Total
1											
2											
3											
4											
5											
6											
7											
8											
9											
10											
11											
12											
13											
14											
15											
16											

Date :	Lanes :

Bowling Score Sheet

Name	1	2	3	4	5	6	7	8	9	10	Total
1											
2											
3											
4											
5											
6											
7											
8											
9											
10											
11											
12											
13											
14											
15											
16											

Date :	Lanes :

Bowling Score Sheet

Name	1	2	3	4	5	6	7	8	9	10	Total
1											
2											
3											
4											
5											
6											
7											
8											
9											
10											
11											
12											
13											
14											
15											
16											

Date :	**Lanes :**

Bowling Score Sheet

Name	1	2	3	4	5	6	7	8	9	10	Total
1											
2											
3											
4											
5											
6											
7											
8											
9											
10											
11											
12											
13											
14											
15											
16											

Date :	Lanes :

Bowling Score Sheet

Name	1	2	3	4	5	6	7	8	9	10	Total
1											
2											
3											
4											
5											
6											
7											
8											
9											
10											
11											
12											
13											
14											
15											
16											

Date :	Lanes :

Bowling Score Sheet

Name	1	2	3	4	5	6	7	8	9	10	Total
1											
2											
3											
4											
5											
6											
7											
8											
9											
10											
11											
12											
13											
14											
15											
16											

Date :	Lanes :

Bowling Score Sheet

Name	1	2	3	4	5	6	7	8	9	10	Total
1											
2											
3											
4											
5											
6											
7											
8											
9											
10											
11											
12											
13											
14											
15											
16											

Date :	Lanes :

Bowling Score Sheet

Name	1	2	3	4	5	6	7	8	9	10	Total
1											
2											
3											
4											
5											
6											
7											
8											
9											
10											
11											
12											
13											
14											
15											
16											

Date :	Lanes :

Bowling Score Sheet

Name	1	2	3	4	5	6	7	8	9	10	Total
1											
2											
3											
4											
5											
6											
7											
8											
9											
10											
11											
12											
13											
14											
15											
16											

Date :	Lanes :

Bowling Score Sheet

Name	1	2	3	4	5	6	7	8	9	10	Total
1											
2											
3											
4											
5											
6											
7											
8											
9											
10											
11											
12											
13											
14											
15											
16											

Date :	Lanes :

Bowling Score Sheet

Name	1	2	3	4	5	6	7	8	9	10	Total
1											
2											
3											
4											
5											
6											
7											
8											
9											
10											
11											
12											
13											
14											
15											
16											

Date :	Lanes :

Bowling Score Sheet

Name	1	2	3	4	5	6	7	8	9	10	Total
1											
2											
3											
4											
5											
6											
7											
8											
9											
10											
11											
12											
13											
14											
15											
16											

Date :	Lanes :

Bowling Score Sheet

Name	1	2	3	4	5	6	7	8	9	10	Total
1											
2											
3											
4											
5											
6											
7											
8											
9											
10											
11											
12											
13											
14											
15											
16											

Date :	Lanes :

Bowling Score Sheet

Name	1	2	3	4	5	6	7	8	9	10	Total
1											
2											
3											
4											
5											
6											
7											
8											
9											
10											
11											
12											
13											
14											
15											
16											

Date :	Lanes :

Bowling Score Sheet

Name	1	2	3	4	5	6	7	8	9	10	Total
1											
2											
3											
4											
5											
6											
7											
8											
9											
10											
11											
12											
13											
14											
15											
16											

Date :	Lanes :

Bowling Score Sheet

Name	1	2	3	4	5	6	7	8	9	10	Total
1											
2											
3											
4											
5											
6											
7											
8											
9											
10											
11											
12											
13											
14											
15											
16											

Date :	Lanes :

Bowling Score Sheet

Name	1	2	3	4	5	6	7	8	9	10	Total
1											
2											
3											
4											
5											
6											
7											
8											
9											
10											
11											
12											
13											
14											
15											
16											

Date :	Lanes :

Bowling Score Sheet

Name	1	2	3	4	5	6	7	8	9	10	Total
1											
2											
3											
4											
5											
6											
7											
8											
9											
10											
11											
12											
13											
14											
15											
16											

Date :	Lanes :

Bowling Score Sheet

Name	1	2	3	4	5	6	7	8	9	10	Total
1											
2											
3											
4											
5											
6											
7											
8											
9											
10											
11											
12											
13											
14											
15											
16											

Date :	Lanes :

Bowling Score Sheet

Name	1	2	3	4	5	6	7	8	9	10	Total
1											
2											
3											
4											
5											
6											
7											
8											
9											
10											
11											
12											
13											
14											
15											
16											

Date :	Lanes :

Bowling Score Sheet

Name	1	2	3	4	5	6	7	8	9	10	Total
1											
2											
3											
4											
5											
6											
7											
8											
9											
10											
11											
12											
13											
14											
15											
16											

Date :	Lanes :

98959186R00057

Made in the USA
Lexington, KY
11 September 2018